Switches and Syrup Sandwiches

Funny, Heartwarming Tales of Childhood in Terrell, Texas

Drew Williams

Backintyme
Palm Coast, Florida, U.S.A.

Copyright © 2006 by Backintyme,
A subsidiary of Boxes and Arrows, Inc.
ALL RIGHTS RESERVED
Backintyme Publishing
30 Medford Drive
Palm Coast FL 32137-2504

phone: 386-446-4909
fax: 206-350-1439
web: http://backintyme.com/publishing.htm
email: sales@backintyme.com
Printed in the United States of America
First Printing, June 2005

ISBN: 0-939479-24-9

Library of Congress Control Number: 2006927563

Contents

Preface 1

Introduction 5

In The Beginning 7

The Little Ones 11

Say What? 13

Ju-Jus Just Ain't What They Use To Be! 17

Me Superman, You Joker 21

Half-Grown People 23

The Fire (Ant) Fighters 27

What Do You Want To Be When You Grow Up? 31

I've Got To Be Me! 33

Silence Is Golden 37

Gone Fishing 41

Heaven Must Be Missing An Angel 43

A Letter To My Grandparents 47

Switches and Syrup Sandwiches

To my son Andrew,

Cousins Brittany, Angel, Alexander, and

Niece Karla.

We hope your children

Will share our memories

Preface

We all rely on our childhood memories to help us rear our children. However, few people can accurately reflect what life was really like for them many years ago. As a matter of fact, the phrase "many years ago" encompasses the time period when our grandparents grew up. Heaven forbid that we would be simple-mined enough to ask a dumb question like the one just posed by your brilliant five year old: "Dad, did you have lanterns or light bulbs when you were a kid?"

As you listen to the question, first in astonishment, then amazement, you think about the time the old man asked the young boy how old he was and the young boy replied that he was five.

In return, the young boy asked the old man how old he was and the old man replied with a question, "How old do you think I am?"

The young boy innocently replied, "I don't know, but you look like you should have been dead a long time ago!"

You ask yourself, "Where in the world do these kids get these million dollar questions from?"

Whether you want to admit it or not, every adult's childhood is considered a long time ago. In their minds you're just an old fart who can't remember which side of the bed you woke up on. It's quite possible your child has identified you as the missing link in the evolution process (Bigfoot). If this raises your eyebrow, check this out. By the time your kids become teenagers you've graduated from climbing trees to just being the old couch potato. As far as they are concerned you haven't been keeping up with the times. No matter how many brain cells you burn trying to figure it out; your kid will never let you escape the old times. Would you like to know where this stuff comes from?

Well, it comes from us. Surely, you remember all those times you felt compelled to share the "good old days" with your children. Did you not feel obligated to tell your youngster what life was like when you were a child?

"Son, when I was a boy, I walked two miles to school every day. It was so cold in the winter I ran most of the way."

Now there you have it! Your child is confused! Right now he's wondering why you didn't take the horse.

"Dad, I thought you said you had a horse. Why didn't you ride the horse?"

The sad thing is he doesn't want to hear that story again. But, when your child breaks a window or something like that, a family story can become quite interesting to them. Now I'm no different from any other parent. I too have been blessed with the age old curse, "I hope you have one just like you!" Parents, you know what I'm talking about. I mean, whoever invented this curse probably encountered more difficulty in raising children than God had with Adam and Eve. But remember there is a light at the end of the tunnel.

Eventually, your child will come to you at some point in their life and ask your old and their new million-dollar question.

When the child asks, you should have an updated answer waiting in the back of your mind: "My child, we used a battery operated lantern with a screw-in light bulb."

Introduction

It was a late summer evening in 1991. My five-year-old son came from Texas to join me in Kansas for the summer. Our normal routine to close out the evening hours consisted of relaxing on the patio, talking about the things we did that day, and discussing the plans for tomorrow. However, this particular evening was different.

Earlier that afternoon, my son and I competed in a game of karate. My son accidentally landed a devastating flying kick to my nose while I was attempting to recover from a fall. My nose didn't bleed; however, it felt as if someone tried to drive a truck through it. Later, as we sat on the patio I couldn't help but to continually look down to see if the swelling had stopped.

"Why are you looking down?" My son asked.

"Son, I'm checking the ground to see if there are any bugs around," I replied.

I'm sure he suspected that he had gotten the best of me. His facial expressions seemed to indicate that the predator had conquered the prey.

As the sun began to creep below the treetops, we became quiet and listen to the sounds of the crickets. It was a relaxing sound. The type of sound that prompted me to reflect on the days gone bye.

My son asked, "Dad, did you have this much fun when you were a kid?"

I replied, "Son, let me tell you about..."

In The Beginning

I was raised in the small town of Terrell, Texas. It wasn't a very large town. You know, "blink an eye and miss downtown!" Still, it was home and as a kid it was everything. The city itself was separated by the railroad tracks. White people stayed on the north side and black people stayed on south. I guess back in the sixties it wasn't considered unusual for a town to be of that stature.

My mother, three older brothers, and one older sister lived in a house located by the black baseball park. Over time it would be torn down and replaced with a basketball court. My father's family owned the house and it was located down the street from my grandparent's house.

My grandparents, T.P. and Exia Malone, were very proud and honest people. We (the grandchildren) called them Daddy and Madear because that's what our parents called them. Madear is short for "my dear." I'm not quite sure how or when the two words became one but it's perfectly obvious we didn't quite get it. Anyway, Madear means the same as Nanna, Big Momma, etc.

They had seven children. While each aunt and uncle that I knew during my childhood held a special place in my heart, Aunt Ida and Aunt Shug would be the ones whose intricate qualities would serve as the center of our activities.

Helen, commonly known as Aunt Shug, was crazy. But don't worry about that now. We'll get to her later.

My grandparents were many things to many people in the community. But, most of all they were my world.

Daddy was a hard working man that believed in taking care of his family. He was fairly tall, average weight, and a great storyteller. Daddy's bark was worst than his bite. He never used profanity around us but his vivid use of metaphors usually gave you a good idea how he felt. "You trifling scamp" and "You no good rascal" normally meant you were less than two minutes away a belt whipping.

Madear was very religious, short, pudgy, and a fantastic singer. Madear had a special gift. She always seem to catch you in the act of committing a wrongful deed and then enjoyed watching you try to squirm your way out of her direct line of questioning.

Unlike Daddy, Madear used a switch. The beginning and the end of a whipping usually went like this:

"Boy, did you break that glass?"

Normally, you would answer, "No Madear, it wuttin me."

Then she would reply, "Ok, go get me a switch so I can whip you for lying!"

During the whipping she would say, "I guess you don't believe fat meat is greasy! Do you?" That was a question I never answered. You know, it could have been a trick question.

This brief encounter would immediately prompt the consoling party to go to the kitchen to make a snack for himself. The syrup sandwich was the "ultimate cheeseburger" for us. Baloney being the "ultimate bacon cheeseburger." That's what our lives consisted of— switches and syrup sandwiches!

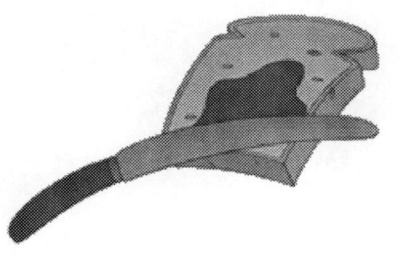

Daddy's yard served as a focal point for most family activities. The front driveway was made of thousands and thousands of sharp tiny rocks. Since all the kids ran around barefooted, the driveway became a major obstacle to overcome. Daddy said the rocks would prevent the kids from running in and out of his front door. Although the sharp rocks didn't bother me, the other kids could only tiptoe across them.

The front and back yard had trees (fruit bearing and non-fruit bearing), a swing, and a bunch of chickens every now and then (depending on the season). On one side of the house was a small field where we played softball. Everything we needed to keep us occupied could be found at Daddy's place.

On the other side of the softball field lived Mrs. Adkins and her two daughters (Chan and Recie). They had a large mutt named Ole Sallie who loved to chase us down the street. In the mornings, I always prayed that Ole Sallie was asleep, eating or doing something else as opposed to providing me with a morning run. Ole Sallie spent half the day chasing cars and kids. The rest of the time she spent wandering from yard to yard. Occasionally, she would wait in the bushes to chase an unsuspecting victim. Every now and then she could be found in Daddy's backyard pulling Madear's freshly washed underwear from the clothesline.

The Little Ones

My older brothers were by far unique in their own special way. My older sister, Cheryl, was no doubt what kids today would refer to as a terminator. Even up until today I still wonder if she hated kids or just couldn't stand the sight of kids getting away with things.

Aunt Jeanie had two kids: Sandra and Bobby Joe. Sandra had a pretty face; two buck teeth and body like a stick. We called her Beamie, because she was as skinny as a beam of light. She was gullible and naïve to the extent that her innocence always put her in the middle of most practical jokes. Bobby Joe on the other hand lived in a world by himself. He was the hero. His character was molded by the things he saw on television. He would never be caught in a supporting cast role as we played throughout our childhood.

Aunt Ida, Aunt Shug, and Cheryl were teenagers. We referred to them as the "half grown people." "Half grown people" were considered both angels and monsters because of their different personalities. Today, we know it as multiple personalities.

Robert, Beamie, Bobby Joe, and I was born between the years 1959 and 1961. We were the youngest in the family for a number of years; thus, we were labeled "The Little Ones." Somehow, the older folks always managed to keep us in the same general area most of the time. It was this interaction of young adult mischief and the coagulation of innocent minds that would set the stage in total support of Murphy's Law.

Say What?

As a child I grew up with many nicknames. Rayfell, Ray-Fee Baby, and Jaybird were by far the most commonly used. Due to the unsubstantiated stories surrounding these nicknames, I will refrain from revealing their origins by parties known or otherwise. However, I will reveal that the names were given by the "half grown people" and in no way reflect how great I was as a kid!

Whenever someone was mad at me or they felt like being a bully, they would usually call me Jaybird. This particular nickname normally sent me into a fit of rage and uncontrollable emotions. There were times when I would be so mad, I would stutter and bad words would come out of my mouth, "You ...you ... monster! You ... you ... do-do head!" I hadn't learned any real profanity so I did the best I could.

My pronunciation of words was very difficult due to the absence of two front teeth. I hadn't quite perfected the "f, st, and sw" sounds. Cheryl would often provoke a conversational fight just for laughs:

"Hey Jaybird, say 'switch'," Cheryl demanded.

"Fitch." I would reply.

"Ok, say 'street'." Cheryl demanded once again.

"Freet!" I would reply.

"Oh, that's good Jaybird," she would say laughingly. "Now say 'fish'!"

I would reply, "Bish!"

By this time she would be laughing so hard that my temper erupted. "Leave me alone!" I screamed.

Then she would grab me and shove me into a corner, "Say 'street' again! Say it! Say it!"

I screamed, "Let me go! Let me go! You horse! You ... you ... monster. Do-do head!"

After I began to stutter, Cheryl was usually content with her daily laugh and walked away. Sometimes I wonder if she did this because she lacked having something else to do. Although I was on the receiving end of someone's mischief, I also knew how to dish it out. Of course, Beamie was my prime candidate. It was like luring the lamb in for the kill with a slab of bacon. One particular story involved the launching of the jets.

During the day I would go to the park and collect empty snow-cone cups. I would fill them with sand and throw them in the air. The sand would flow out the back like the fumes from a jet. It was really fun. So, one day I took Beamie with me to launch the jets. She thought it was really nice since I had already filled the cups with sand. All she had to do was throw them. I threw the first one up in the air and the show began! It was perfect. The sand flowed from the back of the cup and landed on the road.

I handed her the next one. She threw it high in the air and it let out a fine stream of sand. When she walked over to pick it up, she noticed a red color at the tip of the cup. She picked it up and poured out the contents. A frog fell out and began to hop away.

She began to yell and cry, "Rayfell! You put a frog in there!"

I didn't mean to make her so upset but when that spit stuff started coming out of her nose I had to laugh.

I said laughingly, "Beamie, you ... you ... mean you didn't know?"

Beamie is not as sweet and innocent as you may think. Read on a little further and you'll see what I mean.

One morning, Bobby Joe, Beamie, and I played in Daddy's front yard. We had placed several empty coke bottles in the street and we were using them for target practice. It was a rock throwing contest and the competition was fierce. Bobby Joe was ahead. I was in second. Beamie started to cry because she was so far behind. Bobby Joe and I laughed.

Minutes later, we heard Beamie shout, "Bobby Joe! Rayfell! Daddy don't want y'all throwing those rocks." He's gonna get y'all!"

Bobby Joe and I turned toward each other with a look of confusion on our faces. We had no idea that Daddy was lurking to our rear. However, Beamie knew he was coming.

Then we heard Beamie again, "Daddy! Bobby Joe and Rayfell were throwing the rocks from your driveway out into the street! I tried to tell them not to do it! They justa hard-headed!"

Daddy screamed, "You little rock throwing scamps! Didn't you hear Beamie tell ya'll not to throw my rocks in the street!"

As Daddy began to remove his belt, thoughts of restarting the day or perhaps being in another land began to entertain my imagination. Happy thoughts, which suddenly went away with the stinging taste of the Here and Now!

Ju-Jus Just Ain't What They Use To Be!

Cheryl is what I considered a tornado just waiting to hit the ground. She was crazy and mean. Some say she inherited these traits. However, I knew the truth! Cheryl only acted this way when us kids were around. There were times when she was the best sister in the world. Then, there were times when she really showed her true colors. For example, Cheryl made a delicious chocolate cake for us. The big surprise was the cake was made of rubber. But that was ok because we cut it up and threw pieces at each other.

She wasn't much for household chores even though she had more assigned then anyone else in the house. On top of this she couldn't stand to see Bobby Joe or me get away with so many things. Therefore, her wrath was focused on us whenever adult supervision was not present.

Across from our house was a persimmon tree. Anyone who has ever eaten a persimmon knows that a ripe one really tastes good. However, a non-ripe persimmon will make your face shrivel up like a prune. Additionally, a delicious ju-ju berry looks like a non-ripe persimmon.

One morning Bobby Joe and I decided to lay Cheryl's wrath to rest. We picked a bunch of non-ripe persimmons and put them in two bags. Then we picked a couple of ju-ju berries to use for bait. Then we headed for the house. When we arrived, Cheryl was sitting on the couch watching television. We calmly sat on the couch and threw a couple of ju-ju berries in our mouths.

"Umm, these ju-ju berries are so good, ain't they Rayfell!" Bobby Joe said.

I replied, "yea, they taste real good!"

Cheryl's attention immediately turned from the TV and focused on us.

"Y'all give me those ju-ju berries!" she yelled.

As she jerked the bags from us, Bobby Joe screamed, "But Cheryl, those are our ju-ju berries!"

Cheryl reached in the bag, grabs a couple of non-ripe persimmons, and threw them in her mouth. Seconds later, she looked like a big brown prune.

Bobby Joe and I let out a loud laugh and ran through the door like a couple of jackrabbits. As we ran down the street, we could hear the voice of revenge echoing through the trees, bellowing what we believed to be much like the devil himself:

"I'm going to get you! Wait till I get my hands on you!"

When we reached Daddy's front yard, we sat down on the swing to catch our breath.

I looked at Bobby Joe with a smile and said, "You …you …think she liked them ju-ju berries?"

We laughed again.

Switches and Syrup Sandwiches

Me Superman, You Joker

Bobby Joe can best be described as a superhero. His childhood revolved around being the man in charge, the good guy, and the person who could do no wrong. He really believed this was his destiny. As part of his superhero mentality, he sought to protect the innocent and lead the way through dangerous adventures in Daddy's back yard.

His personal demeanor was by far the most visible of all. He was every bit the superhero you see on TV these days. Whenever he lost verbal confrontations, his intellectual behavior rescinded, and his physical superhuman characteristics became apparent. His eyes would become tight, his breathing heavy, and his body muscles flexed.

When the moment was right, he would let out a loud yell, "Aaaaaah!" and charge you like a mad dog. "Aaaaaah!" served as a warning of things to come—the famous death grip. Most people today refer to this type of grip as a chokehold.

Uncle Frank always compared Bobby Joe's death grip to that of an alligator. Eventually, Uncle Frank named him "Baby Alli" (short for alligator). Later we gave him the name "Alligator Man." There were times when he and I had verbal battles. I always got the better of him by calling him "Alligator Man." When he yelled, "Aaaaaah" I would take off running for the rocky driveway. As usual, he would stop chasing me at the driveway because the rocks hurt his feet.

Then my verbal assault would continue, "Alligator Man, Alligator Man! You ... you want some water to swim in?"

As with any predator who has been out-witted, he would stand there and stare. He would stand there for a long time, eyes tight, waiting for you to come out of the rocks. Eventually, he would get tired of waiting and leave. As I departed from the safe haven of the driveway, I could always feel those tight eyes watching me and just waiting for the perfect opportunity for revenge.

Half-Grown People

As I mentioned before, Aunt Shug was crazy. That may be an understatement. She was funny when she was happy, funny when she was sad, and funny the rest of the time. She always made you laugh when you were not the subject of one of her pranks.

Aunt Shug's best friend was Chan. In the morning, you could hear her and Chan conducting their morning ritual, which signified the start of a new day. What ritual you ask? Let's see. Aunt Shug would let up the kitchen window and loudly chirp, "Oouh-ou-Op!" Then Chan would open their kitchen window and respond, "Oouh-ou-Op!" They sounded a lot like two birds looking for a mate. Then they would scream out yesterday's gossip.

As a kid you couldn't slip much pass her. Whether it was the truth or a lie Aunt Shug had one response for your answer. She always looked at you as if she were a detective trying to solve a crime and you were the main suspect.

She would look at you with her cold steel eyes and say, "Ah boy! Stop lying! You don't know what you're talking about!"

Aunt Shug's investigative techniques were identical to Madear's techniques. However, she never whipped us when we were wrong. She conducted corrective training, i.e., joining her new club for a fee. If memory serves me correctly, she owned about 10 clubs. One club for every thing you did wrong.

Beamie was Aunt Shug's and Cheryl's pet peeve when it came to practical jokes. Beamie had an uncontrollable fear of chickens. Aunt Shug and Cheryl knew it.

One evening, Beamie and I were playing on Daddy's swing. All of a sudden, Aunt Shug and Cheryl began a frantic call for help. When we heard it, Beamie immediately jetted for Daddy's backyard to help. Seconds later, Beamie discovered Aunt Shug and Cheryl had gathered all the chickens and were herding them toward her. Beamie tried to reverse her direction but it was too late. She couldn't out run the chickens.

She began running in place and yelling at the top of her lungs, "Help me! Oh, somebody make them go away!"

Of course, Aunt Shug and Cheryl were laughing at the poor little girl conducting running drills in the midst of a bunch of smelly chickens.

Aunt Shug did have a good side. She found very creative ways to keep us occupied when the real grown-ups were away. She was President and Owner of the Malone Family Club. Its members consisted of her, Cheryl, my older brothers, and the four little "dumb" ones. Dumb in the sense that a dime is worth less than a nickel because a nickel is much bigger! At least that's what she told us. Later, she expelled my older brothers for not meeting their daily financial obligations to the club.

What did we get for our money? We got chased around the house three times a week by Aunt Shug (while she held a freshly plucked chicken in her hands and imitated the sounds SQUAWK! SQUAWK! SQUAWK!); we were kept informed on all the daily gossip (of people we didn't know); and finally, we learned all the latest dance moves and developed our rhythm (we never figured out which beat they were talking about).

The Fire (Ant) Fighters

Robert was poetry in motion. Slow motion that is! Everything he did occurred at a snail's pace. He talked slowly, moved slowly and worse of all, he reacted slowly. There were times when his bright ideas were fantastic and other times when they were the pits.

The unknown drove Robert's brain. That is, we could never figure out why he did certain things. He sprayed a wasp nest with water one afternoon. Unfortunately, the occupants were not thrilled with his actions. So, the wasps went on the attack! The entire event lasted close to eighteen seconds. Not bad since it took Robert close to fifteen seconds to make it from the back to the front of Daddy's house. Not only did he enjoy the luxury of walking around with two swollen ears, but also having the pleasure of being labeled "Mr. Taterhead."

Another afternoon we had gathered around an ant bed located in the middle of the softball field. We stood there with sticks trying to beat millions and millions of ants to death. As quietly as he stood there swinging his stick like a turtle he slipped away and returned with a gallon of gasoline.

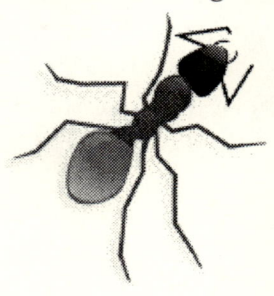

"Here" he said, "pour this on there and throw a match on it."

Being the expert resident firefighter, Bobby Joe quickly took the can and poured it on the ant bed. I threw a match on it and "whoosh!" the bonfire began. After several minutes we discovered not only was the ant bed on fire but the field as well. We attempted to put it out but it was spreading too fast.

Suddenly, we heard the voice of reason, "You low down rascals! What the heck y'all doing out there?"

Bobby Joe shouted, "Oh no! It's Daddy! Run for your lives!"

Daddy ran out of the house to put out the fire. We hid in the weeds hoping to avoid detection.

Daddy screamed, "You trifling scamps come out of those weeds! Get over here! Robert, I saw you running in those weeds! The rest of them have to be with you!"

Bobby Joe should have known you just couldn't trust Robert's bright ideas. The day before, Robert had talked me into starting Madear's old jalopy while the family was in the house.

Robert said, "Rayfell, Daddy and Madear couldn't get the car started this morning. They'll buy us some ice cream if you can start it. Here are the keys. Go out there and start it so they can go to town."

So, I went outside, jumped in and started the car. The car shook so badly it felt like a tornado was coming. I jumped down to push the gas and jump back up to feel the real thrill of the rocking motion. All of a sudden, Aunt Shug and the rest of the family ran out the house. Due to all the confusion I accidentally knocked the gear in reverse and the car backed into the ditch. When it stopped, I jumped out and ran down the street.

I spent the rest of that day visiting other neighborhoods. I came home after dark. I turned off the lights and slipped into bed without any confrontations. Minutes later, the aroma of a freshly plucked switch entered the room!

What Do You Want To Be When You Grow Up?

Most kids grew-up having memories of someone special who provided services. Sure there's Santa Claus, the Tooth Ferry, the Easter Bunny and so on. But, how many of you have ever had a Do-Do Man?

What? You never heard of the Do-Do Man! Well, he was exactly what the name depicts. He was an elderly man who drove a dirty white truck. The Do-Do Man was snaggle tooth like me, which led me to believe I would someday grow up to be one. A thought I hated to even think about and believe me I thought about it a lot.

The Do-Do Man cleaned "outhouses" for a living. When he drove up in his truck we would follow behind him screaming as if he was driving an ice cream truck,

"Do-Do Man! Do-Do Man! Madear, the Do-Do Man is here! Can we help you today?"

But just like good old Saint Nick, he spoke not a word, but went straight to his work. He spoke to everyone and thanked every customer for their business.

I've Got To Be Me!

Although Daddy's yard contained many trees, there was one tree in particular that commanded your attention. The tree stood about forty feet high and its branches extended over large portions of the backyard. As you would stand and look at this tree you could see it was a strong tree. So was the person who fell out of it. I used the singular tense because only one person in the family kept falling out of this tree, Bobby Joe. The boy fell so many times you would think the tree was holding a grudge against him.

One afternoon, Beamie, Bobby Joe, and I climbed about ten feet high in the tree. We had tied Daddy's garden hose to a branch so we could swing down onto a clearing in the yard. Of course a story like this usually depicts a movie or show. You got it, Tarzan. Earlier, we had argued about who was going to be Tarzan, Jane, and Cheetah. As you probably have guessed, Bobby Joe assumed the role of Tarzan, Beamie was Jane, and I had to settle for the lesser of the homosapien species. I was not a happy camper; however, I remained a team player. The key to making a successful swing was the voice imitation of your character's role. If any of you watched the old Tarzan movies then you know Cheetah never did a thing as he swung through the trees. I was not ready to submit to swinging ten feet out of a tree without doing something. Bobby Joe and Beamie had already practiced their yells, which made me even more upset.

In the movies, Cheetah always was the last to swing, but Bobby Joe insisted that I go first. As I swung, I let out the old Tarzan yell, "Auh-Auh-Uh-Auh-Uh!" I made a perfect landing. I grinned because Bobby Joe would be upset with me for doing his yell. As I threw the hose up to Beamie, I notice Bobby Joe's teeth were tightly clinched together. Obviously, he was a little upset.

Beamie began, "Auh-Auh-Uh-Auh-Uh!" She made a beautiful landing. She smiled and threw the hose up to Bobby Joe. As soon as the hose was in his grasp, he became Tarzan. He stood up freely on the branch as if it was the ground under his feet. He proclaimed, "I am Tarzan! King of the

Jungle!" His eyes became tense as if he were in a trance. He took a deep breath and clinched his teeth, "Auh-Auh-Uh-Auh-Aaaaaah!"

The hose broke! Beamie and I watched as Bobby Joe rolled around in the dirt.

Bobby Joe moaned, "Ooh, Ooh, Rayfell, Beamie, Ooh!" We knew he was only finishing out his acting role. While we stood there laughing, Bobby Joe jumped up and charged, "Aaaaaah!"

We took off running for the driveway with Bobby Joe hot on our heels. His eyes were filled with fire and his grasp only inches away from Beamie. But as luck would have it, we reached the rocky driveway and Bobby Joe stopped the chase.

Take into consideration Bobby Joe broke his arm, sprained his ankle, and suffered from a concussion from falling out of this tree. However, he still had not learned his lesson so let me give you one more for the road.

Bobby Joe and I stood on a long branch that was about eight feet high. The branch towered over a pile of old roof tin. The tin represented the alligator pit. The plan was to crawl on your belly the full length of the branch. Finally, drop onto the clearing at the end of the branch.

As I started to crawl, I notice the branch was very strong. It barely shook as I moved across it. I made it over the alligator pit and dropped quietly to the ground. Bobby

Joe began his crawl with as much intensity as he had any other tree adventure. His handgrip on the branch was comparable to the grip of a pair of vise grip pliers. His body laid flat and his feet clung to the branch. Now, keep that thought in mind because once he was positioned over the alligator pit, "Crack! Aaaaaah! Blam!" The branch broke at the base of the tree. His body still clung tightly to the branch and the alligators were having lunch today.

Immediately after this event, Daddy's chickens started to disappear. Later, some were found tied up in the trees along with Bobby Joe's action figures placed there to guard them. Even today, he refuses to divulge any new information. But Daddy knew the truth.

Daddy shouted, "Bobby Joe! If you didn't do it, then tell me who did? Can you explain why I found your GI Joe tied around the neck of one of my chicks? Why is my rooster buried in the ground with only his head sticking up?"

Bobby Joe replied, "Daddy, it wasn't me! It was the alligators!"

Silence Is Golden

There's a lot to be said about having Robert, Beamie, or Bobby Joe as trusted allies. As a matter of fact, anyone who got in trouble as much as we did deserved to have some sort of savior to rely on. Depending on the time of day, we were our own best friends and our own worse enemies. Beamie, bless her soul, never pulled a practical joke on anyone. However, she definitely knew how to get even.

Daddy says our childish pranks create unavoidable circumstances. He called it a "Kush."

He explained it like this, "It's when one of you little knuckle heads get yourself into something you can't get out of. Ain't nothing you can do about it. Just weather the storm until help comes."

I've had my share of kushes in my time. The one that I remember the most is the poison ivy adventure. Man, I'm still itching from that one.

It happened one morning while Beamie and I played in Daddy's front yard. The sun had rose early that morning and the temperature was near 85 degrees. As you can probably guess, it was time for a snow-cone. But, there was one problem. We had no money.

Beamie said, "Rayfell, I know where some people dropped some money last night. Right over there in those bushes. I know they didn't find all of it because they were there a long time. I'll race you over there! Ready, set, go!"

Boy, I ran over there like I was shot out of a cannon. I open my mouth, let out a loud yell, "Aaaaaah," and fell headfirst in the bushes. I tried to cover most of the bushes to keep Beamie from finding any lost coins. I was crawling my way through the jungle-like setting like a piglet in the mud. It wasn't long before I notice I was the only one there. I stopped for a second to peak my head above the leaves. Beamie was still on the other side of the street. I began to wonder why she was grinning. Then it happened.

My body began to itch all over! "Aaaaaah! It's poison ivy," I screamed. I couldn't get up, crawl out, or think of what I should do. Folks, I was stuck in a Kush ... Bad! I was kicking so hard the leaves and rocks were flying in the air.

First I heard Daddy's voice, "Rayfell! Boy what the heck you screaming for! Rayfell! Get your trifling butt out of that poison ivy! Boy! You hear me talking to you?"

Then I heard Beamie's voice, "Daddy! Daddy! Rayfell was out there playing in that poison ivy. I tried to tell him not to go out there, but he's justa hardheaded!. Now, he's justa out there itching and scratching like a dog with fleas."

Well, it was Daddy to the rescue once again. He came over and pulled me out of the poison ivy. Daddy said in a stern voice, "Boy, go in the house! Tell Madear to put some flour on you!"

As I walked toward the house Beamie grinned and giggled. I looked at her and screamed, "You ... you ... fig teeth! Stick girl ... Stick girl look like a fitch!" Beamie just laughed and laughed.

I always knew Beamie had a mean streak in her. Ask Bobby Joe. She locked him up in the outhouse one day. I would have let him out but she said she would get me if I did. Later, I did work up the nerve to ask her why she locked him up. She answered, "I forgot."

I know you readers out there thought Beamie was innocent. That's why I'm telling you this stuff now. You know, just in case you run into her sometime in the future.

Gone Fishing

Some of the best moments I can remember during my childhood occurred when Madear took us fishing. We had long bamboo fishing poles. The best part was digging up our own worms.

Normally, it took about thirty minutes to drive to the pond and another twenty minutes to shake off the dizziness from Madear's old jalopy. Once we got our bearings we would run through the woods and down the hill to the pond.

Everyone had a special spot to fish from. Bobby Joe always fished from the high weeds. No doubt living out another secret spy mission. Beamie always fished from an open spot in the sun. She didn't care much for catching fish. She liked to play with the minnows. Robert always fished under the shade tree. He thought that when the fish got tired they would swim under the tree to rest. Then he could catch them. I always fished next to Madear. She was a true fisherwoman. Whenever she caught a fish, she would pass me the pole.

One particular day Bobby Joe caught a snake. "Madear! Madear! I caught an electric eel!" Bobby Joe screamed. We dropped everything and ran for the car.

Some years later I returned to that old pond. It had dried up due to the lack of rain. I also found a couple of old bamboo fishing poles and the skeleton of an electric eel that didn't get away!

Madear was truly a special woman. She was a "Jane of all trades and master of none." She was definitely independent and only ask for help when she needed it. She was known for her fairness and her deep love for children. That leads me to the next story.

Heaven Must Be Missing An Angel

Aunt Shug and Cheryl weren't all bad. They did have their moments. There was one sunny afternoon when Aunt Shug and Cheryl had gathered us kids together for a walk in the park. It was a beautiful day. Daddy was relaxing in the house and watching his favorite show on television. Madear was at church.

As we walked toward the swings and merry-go-round, we notice the slide had been broken off the ladder. Beamie and Bobby Joe loved that slide and immediately cried like a litter of pups. I didn't care too much for it. The swing was my favorite.

I started to swing in hopes that Beamie and Bobby Joe would stop whining and try something else. Robert decided to swing next to me. I hated it when he would swing next to me. Robert always tried to hold a conversion, which would take forever to end.

"Rayfell, do you remember when Ole Sallie bit me on the leg last week? Well, I bit Ole Sallie's tail yesterday and she just howled and howled," Robert said.

I thought to myself, "Man, I'll be thirty years old by the time he finished this story!"

Robert continued, "but this morning when I passed by Chan's house, Old Sallie had a big pair of women underwear in her teeth. I thought she was looking for a man-dog."

I responded angrily, "ma ... ma ... maybe she was looking for you! You ... you ... doghead! That's why she bit you last week! She was looking for a slow-man!"

Robert exploded like a volcano. So, at the next opportunity I jumped from the swing and ran for Daddy's driveway. By the time I made it Robert was still at the park. But, something else was more interesting.

Aunt Shug, Cheryl, Beamie, and Bobby Joe were dragging the broken slide to Daddy's yard.

Cheryl said, "Jaybird, com'on and help us with this slide. We're going to tie it against Daddy's barn."

It wasn't long before the slide was placed against Daddy's barn. Aunt Shug grabbed some rope and tied the slide to the top of the barn. Next, we climbed to the top of the barn and drew straws to see who would slide first. This was very exciting for me. It was my first lottery. But, Cheryl decided I would go last since I put in the least amount of work.

Aunt Shug sat on top of the slide and started her decent. By the time she reached the bottom Madear appeared out of nowhere. She grabbed Aunt Shug's arm and started whipping her with a switch that she pulled from the pear tree.

She screamed, "Madear! Ouch! We were just ... Ouch! Trying to have some ... Ouch! Ouch! Fun!"

Of course, Madear was uttering something about fat meat thing but I couldn't quite make out the rest. When Madear finished, she looked up the slide and said, "Ok Cheryl your next! Com'on down cause I got to fix dinner soon!"

Cheryl slipped down the slide very slowly and Madear began the assault. Cheryl's whipping was pretty funny. Cheryl screamed, "Madear! Madear! I won't do it no more! I won't do it no more! Whoo! Madear! You're killing me! Whoo!"

Madear responded, "I know you won't do it no more! I know you won't do it no more! You know why? Cause ain't no more slides left at the park!"

By the time Madear finished, Cheryl had crawled through the berry bush, jumped the alligator pit, and ran into the barn. She knew Madear couldn't follow her there. The barn door was too narrow for her to get through it.

Robert, Beamie, and Bobby Joe were in tears. They were scared out of their skins! They had a right to be concerned. Madear was singing "Precious Lord" and they knew heaven was about to open up! One by one, they slowly inch their way down the slide like angels descending from the sky. I wasn't quite sure how all of this ended. I slipped down the backside of the barn and disappeared in the bushes.

Later, I dared to venture into Daddy's kitchen for a quick snack. Unfortunately, I had to settle for a cold drink. Someone had eaten all the bread. I also notice an empty bottle of syrup on the table.

A Letter To My Grandparents

Dear Daddy and Madear,
Its been quite a long time since you went away but I think of you often. So many times I've reminisced about the days when I was a "Little One" and how much you made my life so happy. The new "Little Ones" are teenagers now. Their behavior hasn't changed much from the ones that you knew. I wish you could be here to see them. They're a mess!

The old home place is still standing. However, time continues to take its toll on the old house. Remember the chanti-berry tree you planted in the front yard? Yea, the one you loved so dearly. Well, it's about twenty to twenty-five feet tall now. A good ten feet taller since you last saw it. The persimmon tree didn't survive past beyond the 1990s and the ju-ju berry trees were cut down. But, there is one thing that has managed to survive through the years and that is my memory of you. How I miss you!

When we talk about the "good ole days" that we shared; our spirits rise in hopes that someday we'll see you again. As each day passes by I come to appreciate the trials and tribulations the both of you encountered in times when most black families struggled to survive day by day. Your children and grandchildren are so proud of you and feel truly blessed that we may claim you as our own. The world may never know about your good deeds, but I will always remember the perfect world that you help to create. For me, the world is a better place because you left it that way.

> Your grandson,
> Raphael

𝕭ackintyme

30 Medford Drive
Palm Coast FL 32137-2504
386-446-4909

To order extra copies of this book, visit
http://backintyme.com/ad249.htm

Our complete line of publications is at:
http://backintyme.com/publishing.htm

Printed in the United States
66106LVS00002B/13-21

9 780939 479245